AF483289

# Breaking Through Learning Disabilities

Glenn Smit

**Believe in Yourself because You are Worth it.**

[CONTINUOUS EFFORT – NOT STRENGTH OR INTELLIGENCE – IS THE KEY TO UNLOCKING OUR FULL POTENTIAL.]

--- WINSTON CHURCHILL ---

The author of this publication has compiled this information to the best of their ability. However, the author does not guarantee the accuracy, suitability, usefulness, or completeness of the content shared.

As a parent/guardian, you as a parent/guardian should always seek professional help in taking steps to make significant changes to help your child achieve and succeed in overcoming the learning obstacles that lie ahead.

Our children are the future ambassadors and leaders of this earth. We must teach them with God's Agape Love and direction to give them the best guidance and support they need.

# Table of Contents:



## Chapter 1

# Chapter 2



# Chapter 3

# Chapter 4



# Chapter 5



# Conclusion

# Acknowledgements:

Before I give my thanks, I want to convey what the Spirit of the Lord imparted to me to share with all readers. Most people will say you give thanks to God, but this book doesn't reveal or acknowledge anything about God's Word.

The truth is that Father's Word should be shown in our lifestyle when we say we are living for God. His Word made flesh (alive) in us. God can use any circumstance, situation, or book like this to manifest His Presence.

It's not about how much effort we make in our walk with God. It's about how we (comply) with His Word to be (renewed and transformed) to be the example in this world the way He intended us to be.

With that said, I want to take a moment to honour our Beloved Father God for the incredible impact He had on me through the good and hard times growing up and continuing to do so to fulfill His Plan and Purpose for my life as His son.

I express my thanks to my family for their love and support. I truly appreciate you have always been there for me when I needed you. Thank you so much!

My sincere gratitude and appreciation go toward my spiritual father, Kobus Swart enlightening, uplifting, and equipping me with God's help on how I need to pursue my mandate and to be an exact representation of Jesus our Lord and King.

I want to thank the Body of Christ, my family in God, for always being authentic, expressing boldness, and for your unconditional love and support throughout my journey in life.

I want to single out a few Christlike friends, Tobie Fourie being the solid pillar he has been in my life and for his tremendous support over the years as a true friend and brother in Christ.

Philip Crafford is another remarkable brother and friend to whom I'm grateful to God and how Father made us connect. Words alone cannot express it. Your support and love throughout our connection are so much appreciated.

Finally, Michelle Swart is a wonderful woman that Father not only brought into my life as a friend but made me embrace as a real sister. This book is inspired not by what you have experienced in life but also by the excellent example you set as a follower of Christ.

# **About The Author:**

Glenn Smit lives in one of the most beautiful remote parts of the world Cape Town, in South Africa. Furthermore, he is an authentic guy with a great sense of humor who enjoys associating with people who show determination, perseverance, and willingness in wanting to learn in their hearts.

Glenn studied through the best Import Export Agency in the world by the name Wade World Trade in UK England, Birmingham. After his studies, Glenn had no work, but eventually helped his Dad in Tiling and later developed a real passion for it.

After a few years, Glenn pursued his own business in SEO (Search Engine Optimization) while doing Tiling part-time and went full-time into SEO afterwards. In this new business venture, Glenn has helped people and businesses how to brand themselves effectively.

The insights and experience he gained through Wade World Trade with hard work and commitment have helped him exceptionally well in wanting to pursue a successful business both on and offline.

Glenn occasionally enjoys playing golf, ten-pin-bowling, and pool when he gets the chance to do so. He is also an avid reader and loves writing, and unexpectedly realizes he would be so devoted to it that he would start to commit himself to write a book.

You will never hear Glenn say he knows it all because he doesn't or is the best because he is not. He is always open and committed to learning.

I admire his motto in business: "People don't join a company, but join you. When you take care of them, they take care of you."

This humble man adores, value, and appreciate all kinds of people and adapt quickly to almost any environment. He is a passionate learner who loves helping people by being a valuable asset wherever an opportunity comes or just being there for people.

# Foreword:

## By: Michelle Swart

Most bookworms have that one book on the bookshelf with the prime position where its only function is to let it gather as much dust as possible. The profound framework of this book was developed ten years ago and was supposed to be published, but things changed.

As the years progressed, God was busy shaping the author further into His Plan and Purposes for his life and eventually reminded him it's time to go to that book, rewrite, upgrade, and make it more significant and relevant to bring complete understanding.

It only was recently awakened that this incredible book brought forth a new lease of life. The author offers readers greater understanding, clarity, encouragement, hope, and support. This informative read aims to provide a deeper understanding of the various aspects of learning disabilities.

Remember, each individual has a unique place as a member of society. Everyone has their distinct character where they can contribute to their full ability. All are extremely valuable!

I firmly believe that everyone should read this nugget. It's not just for people who have (or know) a child with a learning disability. The main goal of this book is to de-stigmatize learning disabilities.

Never make your child feel isolated, alienated, worthless, unlovable, stupid, etc.

Dear Reader, I urge you to be extremely sensitive and

considerate when dealing with a person with a learning disability. Everyone deserves treatment with dignity and respect!

This book should be on every family's bookshelf! May it bring more than just new meaning into your life, but also how you ought to embrace people with learning disabilities. All I ask is, I hope it doesn't use the art of collecting dust!

I pray that this book will leave a lasting impact on readers and will change perspectives and outlooks concerning the world of learning disabilities as a whole.

Enjoy!

**God bless!**

# Introduction

The number of children diagnosed with learning difficulties increases yearly compared to the previous year. Many of these cases happen because "experts" could profit from these diagnoses.

While many experts genuinely care about children's well-being, some misdiagnose many children.

Learning disabilities go beyond the inability to master certain learning areas or behaviors; many refer to other conditions, whether mental illness, behavioral problems, or other disorders related to learning disabilities.

To fully understand learning disabilities, you'll need to research to know what you are dealing with. You should not simply downplay that you or your child may have a learning disability.

This book provides relevant information and research to help you understand learning disabilities, the various types, and how to deal with them accurately and effectively.

**Disclaimer:** The information provided is not by a medical practitioner and is for educational and informational purposes only. The content is not a substitute for professional medical advice, diagnosis, or treatment. If having doubts about a medical condition, always consult your doctor or another qualified healthcare provider. Never ignore medical advice or delay seeking medical attention because of what you read.

Because natural and dietary supplements are not FDA-approved, product labels must carry a two-part disclaimer that the FDA has not evaluated the claim and assure that the product does not intend to "diagnose, treat, cure, or prevent any disease."

# Chapter 1

## What Are Learning Disabilities?

A learning disability is simply thinking differently than others. Many of these minds are particularly gifted in one area and may have difficulty learning in other areas.

When a person has a learning disability, they often have to work harder to understand facts and words. Sometimes people can try too hard. But if there is active persuasion, one is more likely to succeed.

Some people have a learning curve that takes practice that is only natural. However, some people are on a learning curve set by teachers, which only confuses people with learning disabilities.

These people need to learn at their own pace. What happens is that the learning curve they've given confuses them then they can become mentally disabled in certain areas.

Having a learning disability does not necessarily mean that the person cannot learn. They may be slow in one subject area and a fast learner in another.

To correct the problems caused by a learning disability, you need to understand the person as an individual. Individuality is how a person differs physically and mentally, especially in their personality.

Personalities differ from person to person, and they are the brilliance of the social and personal qualities that a person embodies. Personality forms through years of interaction with people. Personality is what makes everyone unique.

The purpose of personality tests is to create, develop and help therapists, counselors, and doctors determine each social and personal characteristic of different personalities. Very few personality tests reveal this.

Some schools will find resources to help them teach children with learning disabilities. Some schools have even begun to work individually with children with learning disabilities and partner with teachers to work directly with these children.

Therefore, a child with a learning disability may have many options, but it may cost more to send the child to these schools, and parents may need more attention to care for their child.

New research and courses are made regularly for these students. Many of these are practical and effective in helping children with learning disabilities.

The new strategy has proven usable for children with ADHD and dyslexia. These phonic strategies are reliable for children with a variety of learning disabilities.

Most schools have established target systems for these children. It helps them achieve their short-term and long-term goals. However, these goals are often too vague for some children.

It is always necessary to help children understand these goals without confusion. Simple language must prompt, as words with large vocabulary can confuse children.

In some cases, children with learning disabilities also have difficulty understanding speech. When the teacher speaks too much vocabulary, the child may become confused. Many children fall into the trap of learning disabilities only to end up with teachers who exacerbate the problem.

Mental health professionals also often over-define learning disabilities. Many people believe that if a person has a mild learning disability, they are a psychopath. In some cases, they are also often over-diagnosed.

For example, many mental health researchers are trying to prevent antisocial personality disorder and psychopathic disorder. It is because even when the labels are accurate, the names can be confusing. Other mental health professionals have difficulty diagnosing multiple personality disorders.

Some people think the disorder is some form of schizophrenia, but that's not the case. Others may believe that the condition borders psychotic schizophrenia, which is far from the truth.

These people tend to be quite intelligent in mental abilities and far exceed their peers. Some people form personalities at the age of one to escape the trauma and abuse they experience.

Learning disabilities are sometimes often made up rather than based on pure facts. When the child can learn, you must look at all the symptoms before making any drastic decisions.

# Causes And Warning Signs Of A Learning Disability

Learning difficulties have many causes that often make it incredibly difficult to pinpoint the exact cause. However, some of these common risk factors can lead to learning disabilities, such as:

-Genetic factors: Learning disabilities can be passed down from parents to children. If your family has a history of learning disabilities, you may be more likely to develop one yourself.

-Premature birth: Babies who are born prematurely or at a low birth weight are more likely to develop learning disabilities.

-Medical problems: certain medical conditions, such as problems with the heart or brain, can lead to learning disabilities.

-Injury: A head injury or other trauma to the brain can cause learning disabilities.

There are a number of warning signs that may indicate a learning disability. These include:

- Struggling to read or write at the same level as classmates

- Frequently losing track of thoughts or forgetting what has been learned

- Difficulty understanding concepts or following instructions

- Avoids or resists reading and writing tasks

- Displays poor organizational skills

- Exhibits low self-esteem or feels overwhelmed by school-
work

# Symptoms of Learning Disabilities

Many symptoms can indicate a learning disability. If your child is struggling at school or has any of the following skills, they may have a learning disability:

-Reading, writing, and spelling
-Math
-Organization and time management
-Reasoning and problem-solving
-Memory

If your child has any of these symptoms, it is vital to have them evaluated by a professional. Only after an examination can a diagnosis be made and an appropriate treatment plan developed.

Several symptoms may indicate a learning disability. Some children however may have difficulty speaking, learning new words, or following directions.

Others may have problems with reading, writing, or math. Some children may have these difficulties at the same time. Many children with learning disabilities also have problems with short-term memory, organization, and attention.

Learning disabilities are more common than we think. The estimate is about 15 percent of people have a learning disability.

Although there are many different types of learning disabilities, they all have one thing in common:

They are hard to diagnose and identify. That's why it's vital to recognize the signs and symptoms of learning disabilities early to get the help your child deserves.

# Getting a Diagnosis for Learning Disabilities

There are several ways to diagnose a learning disability. The most common approach administers a series of tests to individuals to assess various skills such as reading, writing, and mathematics. These tests can help identify areas where a person may have problems.

In some cases, brain imaging techniques, such as an MRI or CT scan, may be used to look for physical abnormalities causing learning disabilities. In other cases, doctors may use genetic testing to look for any genetic mutations that may cause the condition.

Once diagnosed, patients can begin working with a team of specialists to develop a treatment plan that may help them manage their condition better and improve their quality of life.

If you think your child may have a learning disability, the first step is to consult your child's doctor or another healthcare professional.

Learning disabilities are neurological disorders that make it difficult for children to learn and process information. They are not the result of laziness, lack of drive, or intelligence.

Learning disabilities can be diagnosed through a comprehensive assessment by a team of specialists. Assessments typically include:

• A review of your child's medical and developmental history

• One-on-one testing with a psychologist or other trained professional

• Observations of your child in school and at home

• A battery of academic achievement tests

After the assessment, the team will meet with you to discuss their findings and recommendations. If your child has been diagnosed with a learning disability, the team will work with you to develop an Individualized Education Program (IEP). This document will outline the specific services and accommodations your child will need to succeed academically.

# Chapter 2

## Learning Strategies

It can be hard to watch a child struggle with a learning disability, especially if they don't understand why they are struggling. It can lead to depression and even feelings of helplessness. But some strategies can help your child better manage learning difficulties.

These strategies focus on making learning easy and more fun and creating an environment where your child can succeed and feel confident in their abilities. From breaking tasks into smaller chunks to visual aids and more, these proven strategies can help your child unlock their potential. Read on to learn more about how to use them!

Students with learning disabilities often have difficulty understanding. It's because their decoding process is different from other students. Several recent studies have shown how computer-related tools can help children with learning disabilities. Among these tools are prompts combined with word learning systems.

According to most professionals, these obstacles mostly happen and are done by children being too eager to learn words. Other experts believe that mental illness prevents children from learning about their disability.

But the problem often exists between the child as an individual and education. If a child does not understand the meaning of a word, it simply means that he is not clear about the word. It's not always the case for all learning disabilities but in many cases.

For example, when working with a woman with bipolar manic depression, the woman may want to learn. However, she may suffer from extremely low self-esteem and poor self-esteem. These two things will keep her from learning because she doesn't trust herself and her ability to learn.

Therefore, it can be difficult for a woman to learn. All because she doesn't believe in her abilities! This woman has a flawed character that holds her back. So it's not the depression holding her back, but the personality disorder holding her back that's the underlying problem.

Another problem that seems to come up is that some people have a lot of emotional scars. These people let their emotions rule their minds.

It means that they have many stressors that interfere with learning. It also causes constant confusion in their minds, preventing them from learning.

Unfortunately, most mental illnesses have varying degrees of severity and varying symptoms. Some people with bipolar disorder are more severe than others and can learn effectively.

Some people with bipolar disorder cannot understand because they refuse to accept it. This type of patient does not see the importance of learning. They feel like they have nothing to offer at all.

Patients with ADHD (attention deficit hyperactivity disorder) are another area of research. ADHD has long been the focus of much research. These patients often have symptoms such as the inability to concentrate. They also have hyperactive behavior with unusual comments or inappropriate words that can disturb or interrupt others.

Also, patients often do not understand why these actions are not appropriate. These patients tend to hurt other people's feelings and do not seem to care about them. They may also claim to be bored after a short game.

Some of them also rarely show how to focus on one task at a time. It often means they are having trouble concentrating and sitting in front of the computer for long periods. It also shows that phonics may not be for everyone.

Most people diagnosed with ADHD are intelligent people. Their minds are often very active and racing at 144 kilometers per hour, making it difficult to focus.

It means that these individuals do not necessarily need to concentrate. They tend to learn more by observing. Observational learning skills are likely to benefit people with ADHD.

However, this does not necessarily mean that these people do not have learning difficulties. Research also shows that people with ADHD often do best when participating in an individualized learning program. Children with dyslexia also learn better this way.

Children with learning disabilities must be allowed to focus and needs attention individually to learn at their level of understanding. It also helps the child to live with the disability.

# Treatments for Learning Disabilities

5% to 15% of school-age children are estimated to have some part of a learning disorder. Although the exact cause of these disorders is unknown, they are measured to have a neurobiological origin.

There are many different treatments for learning disabilities, and the best approach depends on each child and the severity of the condition that they might have. Some common treatments include:

- Special Education: This is customized education that takes into account the child's learning difficulties. It can be taught in general classes or special schools.

- Behavior therapy: This helps children learn new skills and cope with their disabilities. This can include rewards and punishments to help change behavior.

- Medication: In some cases, medication can help improve concentration. Stimulants are often prescribed to children with attention deficit hyperactivity disorder (ADHD).

- Alternative Therapies: Many alternative therapies are helpful for children with learning disabilities. These include sensory integration therapy, art therapy, and music therapy.

The most common attitude towards learning difficulties is special education. The Special Education Plan is structured to meet the unique needs of each child, which may include a smaller class scale, personal indications, and things that focus on practical learning.

In some cases, medication help manage the symptoms associated with learning disabilities. Stimulant medications treat attention deficit hyperactivity disorder (ADHD), one of the most common co-morbidities in children with learning disabilities. Medicines can also help treat anxiety or depression in children with learning disabilities.

Many children with learning difficulties also benefit from tutoring or other additional education. When you are focused, patient, and committed to helping these kids, it makes progress so much easier.

If you think your child may have a learning disability, you need to talk to your doctor or child's teacher about your concerns. Early diagnosis and intervention will help children with learning disabilities succeed in school and life.

# Learning To Live With Disabilities

If you've been diagnosed with a learning disability, you can choose to accept it and move on, or you can choose to let it get in the way of your life. Being diagnosed with a learning disability does not mean you have a disability.

You may also choose a physical exam and begin to rule out any physical problems. Many mental health professionals and doctors make mistakes, so it doesn't hurt to research and run some medical tests to determine if this learning disability stems from another physical problem.

Therefore, if diagnosed, you want to verify that the diagnosis is valid and not a mistake. Some doctors look for a problem and will create problems where there may not be one.

This situation is not unusual. Other people want to make money from your position. So if you've been diagnosed with a learning disability, it's time to get on Google and do some research.

What if you have a learning disability? Let's say you have ADHD. It is a common disability that people are diagnosed with and can hinder learning. Being diagnosed doesn't mean you can't learn will only take longer.

There are also many different degrees of learning difficulties. Many famous people have also been diagnosed with these disorders, ranging from dyslexia to ADHD and bipolar disorder.

Very few people also have learning disabilities. Many have a mental condition that gets in the way of learning. For example, schizophrenia can also cause learning disabilities but can be treatable.

People with schizophrenia are mentally detached from reality and have difficulty learning because they struggle mentally to overcome mental disturbances such as auditory hallucinations, hallucinations, and delusions.

They may also have frequent delirium. However, these people are capable of learning – they only take longer than others.

People with mental disabilities, formally known as intellectual disabilities, also have learning disabilities. These individuals are capable of learning. Their physical and mental disabilities might make them slow, but they are not incapable of mastering learning.

Other learning difficulties are affected. These people are often called those with histrionic personality types and psychopathy. People with limited personalities also have some learning difficulties. It is because their grandiosity prevents them from seeing the truth.

These individuals are often self-destructive and even suicidal. When you leave them, they don't notice what they are doing. In other words, they are afraid of being abandoned. Because the fear is so overwhelming, nothing matters to them, and their ability to learn is restrained.

Learning disabilities are not always related to mental illness. Learning disabilities are related to cognition, linguistics, and language. If a person has difficulty in these areas, there is usually a good reason.

Unfortunately, unless the mind is required to start learning outside its field of understanding happens. Many people will go into imitation mode. They will begin to copy the rules and guidelines set by their role models. They lose touch with their individuality and start doing what their role models do.

For example, have you ever noticed that all the controlling people in movies follow the same personality type? Because people with controlling personalities learn these behaviors from other people.

A person may consider having a learning disability when they follow a behavior. Unfortunately, so-called "normal" individuals fail to recognize this behavior and change before it gets out of control. If you've been diagnosed with a learning disability, it's important not to give up.

# Strategies for Overcoming Learning Disabilities

Learning disabilities can be a difficult challenge for both children and their parents. Whether it's autism, dyslexia, or another learning disability, providing the best possible education for children with special needs is a real struggle.

There is no one-size-fits-all answer to overcoming a learning disability, as everyone's needs are unique. However, some general strategies can help many people with learning disabilities when helping them the right way.

An important strategy is to find a "learning ally"—who can offer support and understanding and help advocate for your needs. It could be a friend, family member, or teacher.

Also very important to have a strong support network of professionals who can provide advice and guidance, such as an educational psychologist or professional mentor.

Another strategy is to focus on your strengths and use them to compensate for your weaknesses. For example, struggling with reading comprehension, listening to audiobooks, and using text-to-speech software will help. If you struggle with writing, you can focus on developing your oral communication skills.

Ensuring you have the right resources and technology is also very important. Many useful tools and apps make learning easier for people with learning disabilities. Some examples are mind-mapping software, flashcard apps, and text-to-speech software.

Of course, these are just some general strategies—ultimately, you can find what works best for you. The most important thing is to never give up on yourself – with hard work and determination, anything is possible!

# Chapter 3

## Learning Disabilities – A Brief History On Development And Understanding

As children grow, they learn many new concepts and behaviors. In some cases, confusion can occur and prevent the child from learning certain behaviors. Most children can overcome this confusion, but others cannot and have difficulty learning skills.

It is more common in boys because their fathers expect them to learn certain areas quickly. Most fathers don't realize the academic demands they place on their children or what is beneath the surface of their children's brains.

When a child goes to school, the child deals with several different areas of learning. They learn reading, writing, math, science, social studies, and other subjects. Many children will set their own learning goals to accommodate this extra influx of information and become confused.

Children may struggle to learn these subjects because they try to meet the expectations of others, namely parents, especially fathers. Most children will be more scientifically oriented and be confused by the information presented to them by others.

Many children also turn to mathematics because they can see the connection between the two subjects, and most scientific research is on mathematical statistics. Later, the child will start looking for patterns.

For some children, it is one parent. For others, it's the role of television. However, when children learn that TV characters are not apparent or fictional, they begin to look for real-life examples based on the characteristics of their TV role models.

It starts creating confusion in the child's mind as the child cannot find such a person. But children will still look to their parents for this example. Let's say dad has a job demanding a lot of physical activity where he works 50 hours a week.

Every night when he comes home, he is tired. When dad comes home from work, the child begins to notice every detail of how dad behaves. The child then tries to compare him to his TV character to determine if the TV character is fictional. Then the child begins looking for what he wants to be in life.

All these different ideas and comparisons combined with school activities and information become a whirlwind of confusion for the child. Children often forget their struggles and try to please others. Add to this peer pressure from other kids at school.

They tell the child that if they don't want to be like everyone else, they are not normal at all. It's only the beginning and many stages of development of a child with a learning disability.

The term learning disability itself is a bit of an understatement and doesn't fully capture what a learning disability is. After all, we all struggle with some form of learning disability in what we do.

Your math may not be excellent, but your English and art are. Or you might learn something; it requires you to be a little more than everyone else.

This type of learning disability is quite common, very natural, and happens to all in one form or another. The fact that we don't understand as quickly as other people can lead to a person known as having a learning disability when you are not disabled at all.

There are many such examples in life. For example, people with learning disabilities are often called "stupid" or "retarded". Later, through scientific reviews, researchers prove that people with disabilities have a lot to teach us.

Those who were considered retarded or retarded are considered failures, but we now know that many mentally disabled children are very capable of learning. The difference is they learn more slowly and require different teaching methods.

The scientific community still categorizes people with learning disabilities. Many of these are due to psychological conditions, while others are physical conditions that cause disability.

People with mental disabilities learn differently and require different teaching methods. They can still adapt if appropriate training and learning methods are supported.

These people can also contribute a lot to society. These children are not what we just said. These people exist in a different world than the one you and I live in, a place comparable to a reality different from yours.

But throughout history, we have seen people with learning disabilities treated cruelly and even inhumanely. Because of this, even today's kids think there is nothing wrong with treating these kids the same way.

People with developmental disabilities have been ostracized, institutionalized, and often beaten or tortured. Admittedly, this behavior does not happen today, but the negative perception of these people persists, and children are often even crueler to these people, causing emotional pain to the victims.

There are ways to overcome learning disabilities. A simple tool you can use right away is "self-talk." Self-talk can help you discover who they are and what they want to achieve. When people solve problems, they can tell themselves the steps to take so they can focus on the task at hand.

Other skills like observational, investigative, and general self-paced learning can help them start working their way up the learning curve. Studying and gathering evidence is an effective way to learn.

It is also beneficial to learn about different types of teaching methods. Visual, hands-on, auditory, and combinations of these are effective learning methods that you want to discover the easiest way for you or your child to learn.

# Learning Disability Diagnosis Inconsistencies

Children diagnosed with learning disabilities are associated as disabled because they are unable to master certain learning areas or skills. That does not make them disabled at all.

Many children discover a learning difficulty like reading, and you must be patient with them. Some kids have unique learning styles, while others do their best to follow the controlled learning standards set by many schools.

Some people refuse to let other people, such as teachers, political leaders, and other influential people, influence their thinking. Others explore and use their creative thinking; it happens in schools. Those not interested in art, writing, or other creative fields rarely use their creative thinking skills.

As a result, children with mild symptoms of a learning disability are often diagnosed with a learning disability and significantly tortured by a mental health professional in the aftermath.

Mental health professionals are a challenge because their skills vary widely. Some professionals are with you, but their focus is not on you when others are willing to help. Working with therapists and counselors can be frustrating, but once you find someone you become friends with who seems successful, stick with it.

Not all counselors are the same, and many are more concerned with following a code of ethics and what other counselors think is the "normal" or right way to do, rather than letting their intellect guide them in the right direction. This is what makes wiser people diagnosed with a learning disability different from everyone else.

Instead of simply believing and accepting what they learned, they search for information about their condition and look for facts that support their diagnosis. Often these people find the reading material more confusing than informative and notice false facts.

So you have to wonder if the learning disability is failing communication between the child, the tests they took to diagnose the learning disability, the counselor, and their parents.

Communication breakdowns are one of the most common causes of diagnostic errors. A quick look at the history of diagnosing learning disabilities in many countries will give you proof of that.

If you notice, we look for information from history, but we try to live for the future. Anyone who looks back at the school system in a country in the past will see many inconsistencies.

Conflicts also tend to be another big problem in most countries. Children who are less stressed and not exposed to neglect or abuse tend to be less intelligent than those who are. Children with mental illness tend to be more attentive than those who are not.

The actual reason why this happens it's because the child or individual uses knowledge from previous experiences to think at different levels of experience. Unfortunately, mental health professionals and teachers often judge neglected or abused children and claim they are mentally ill.

The fact that the child acts out of a learned behavior rather than mental illness makes more sense. A lot of behaviors have been misdiagnosed by mental health professionals because they are often contradictory.

For example, when therapists notice oppositional traits in a child, they first see the opposition as the cause of the behavior rather than a learned behavior that the child uses to get what they want. Children with the oppositional defiant disorder often struggle against rules prescribed by educational leaders or other leaders in life.

The Opposing Position Recalcitrant patients often become very aggressive when their views and beliefs are in a very demanding position. Sometimes these individuals are relentlessly aggressive toward those they target.

On the other hand, children with oppositional behavior will let that behavior come and go when they need it. This behavior is less common in children with the oppositional defiant disorder. These behavior patterns are patterns that they have learned from their life experiences.

These behaviors are rarely consistent because people can turn them on and off as needed and function normally in society throughout their lives. However, this is most evident in children who have tantrums.

They learned from experience that if they lost their temper in the middle of the grocery store, their mom or dad would buy them a toy or candy to calm them and not cause a scene. What a perfect example of learned oppositional behavior. So, as you can see, learning disabilities are easily overstated.

# Breaking The Stigma Around Learning Disabilities

The stigma associated with learning disabilities is a problem in our society. People affected by learning disabilities are problematic or incapable of success. However, this could not be further from the truth.

Learning disabilities are complex and varied and affect people in different ways. While there is still a long way to go to break down the barriers of learning disabilities and challenge the stigma, it is vital to raise awareness of their existence and understand the reality of living with them.

As you progress further in this book, we will also discuss how to support people and how you can break down the stigma surrounding them that needs to be corrected.

The stigma attached to learning disabilities is that they are a sign of weakness or lack of intelligence. It couldn't be further from the truth! Learning disabilities are neurological differences that affect the way the brain processes information. They do not reflect a person's intelligence or value as a person.

People with learning disabilities often face discrimination and misunderstandings from others. Educating yourself and others about what learning disabilities are and how they affect people is imperative to breaking down these barriers. Here are some facts about learning disabilities:

• Learning disabilities are common and affect one in five people in the world. It does not happen by laziness, bad parenting, or bad teaching. Instead, they have to do with differences in how the brain processes information.

• Most people don't realize that people with learning disabilities often have above-average intelligence. Many famous and successful people have overcome learning disabilities to achieve their goals and dreams with support given to them!

· Learning disabilities can affect any area, from school and work to relationships and daily activities. By understanding and accepting people with learning disabilities, we can help create a more inclusive world for everyone.

# Using Compliments To Help Children With Learning Disabilities

Complimenting children is often the best way to help them learn. Complimenting children with learning disabilities is essential because these people often struggle more than other children. They always have low self-esteem because they feel unreasonable, abnormal, or unpopular in certain situations.

They are often centered and marked differently than other children, and many do not understand why this is so. Moreover, these children are often confused about the different meanings. In short, when they are baffled simple compliments can help them get through the day and complete the learning process.

Being different is a beautiful thing. It means that a person is totally or partially different from others, and different is good. There would be no fun in life if we were all exactly alike.

Everyone will be the same the world will be a miserable place to live. Why would you travel to another country when it looks like yours? Why would you create art if it all looks the same? You don't do that. So it's good to be different.

The problem is that most people are all right with being a different gender, race, and nationality but having a learning disability and being psychologically distinctive, people don't seem to understand and don't want to believe that it's okay to be different.

This mentality of not understanding that being different is good has led to hatred and wars between people. It also meant that many mentally ill or people with a different mentality were tortured and looked down on.

Although this prejudice is not as strong as in previous centuries, it still exists to some extent, and the mentally ill are still subject to persecution. The fact that we are all the same is a fact that no one can or should deny.

Because many people are under-diagnosed with learning disabilities, it's vital to know the terms of it. A learning disability means a person may have difficulty learning a particular subject due to a mental impairment. People with learning disabilities continue to show signs of impairment.

If a person struggles in just one area, they don't necessarily have a learning disability, just a slower learning process in that particular area. When a person doesn't manage with a skill, the material they are learning can be what holds them back.

For example, beliefs that cause confusion, division, and discord happen in religion. Religious people of different sects worship in different ways and teach doctrines that can make learning very difficult.

Religion is the first area that creates the most confusion in a person. For centuries we have been taught that people are born with intuition, but God says otherwise because we are born of the Holy Spirit who lives within us.

Trust in intuition and understanding recedes during life, and the consequences often lead to a disintegration of beliefs over time, which can be a big problem for those unable to resolve these disturbances in their belief system.

As children grow up, many persuasive people and behaviors influence their lives. Many are highly intelligent and can easily observe the consistency of behavior and reactions to that behavior.

For example, children can easily distinguish between good and bad behavior. They will also recognize what these activities involve.

If a child sees another child throwing a tantrum and then rewarded for bad behavior, they will remember this and may try the same tactic with their parents later. When some misbehavior's are given attention to, a child learns which works for them and which doesn't.

If your child has a learning disability and has been diagnosed with a disorder such as ADHD, your child should have regular check-ups. With constant physical therapy, many people with ADHD begin to feel more focused in life.

The Diagnostic and Statistical Manual of Mental Disorders IV was correct when it first published information linking ADHD to the central nervous system.

However, the diagnostic symptoms of the condition are usually psychiatric illnesses and learning disabilities. So it's important to remember that healthcare professionals find their answers, and remembering this as a parent can help you find the answers for your child.

It's also important to recognize that many conditions have overlapping symptoms, so you shouldn't focus on just one area when there might be other conditions interacting in the mind and body.


You will never give up on a child who works hard. The best thing you can do for them is to find the answers yourself and help them. If your child is well treated, don't believe everything you hear. Please commit to investigating when children who are not allowed to study will have learning disabilities.

# Don't Keep Your Child From Learning

As a parent or teacher of a child with learning disabilities, the worst thing you can do is prevent them from learning. Learning difficulties are often associated with mental disorders, stress, anxiety, and other phobias. When children are diagnosed with a learning disability, they get moved away from learning what they are capable of doing.

Many children will struggle quietly throughout school and hide the fact that they are struggling academically. Some students are often able to hide their learning disabilities by pretending or simply avoiding situations where they will discover that they lack skills. On the other hand, some children will act and ask for help. Other children show their incompetence through inappropriate behavior.

An example of this is a young boy struggling to control his behavior. Many diagnosed the boy with several dangerous conditions, but teachers often noticed that when they played along with he worked better and did better.

Most teachers thought he was a bright student, even though he failed in many aspects of school. After everyone stopped bullying him, the kid got good grades and did well. It's the incredible power of peer pressure. Peer pressure can hinder a child's learning.

In some cities, many children escape peer pressure by joining gangs or simply dropping out of school. It is much easier for them to give up than to be teased by a learning disability. Children are also more likely to drop out of school to avoid peer and peer pressure.

Many teachers do not get progress from these children because they do not feel that these children do not want to grow, and their efforts are not worth it. These kids usually are thrown into societal molds as losers, gang members, and deviants.

Children want to learn but can't handle the pressure from teachers and other students. Instead of looking for answers and trying to help these children, teachers pull them out of school and onto the streets to get an education. As you can see, banning children from learning simply does not work.

Many children are delayed in their studies because they do not achieve the results expected before moving on to the next grade. It also makes these children feel depressed and stressed. It makes them feel like failures and often causes them to drop out of school.

However, other kids are good at faking their abilities and working the system to succeed in school. Instead of seeing their situation negatively, they can persevere with their studies in school.

People with learning disabilities often struggle to understand themselves. Many people will take the words of experts as gold and not seek the truth.

Often parents sit back and watch their children's lives controlled by doctors and therapists instead of seeking answers themselves. Instead of looking for the answers that might work for their child, they tend to wait for others to provide them.

Children want to learn. They want to know and want to learn just like everyone else. They want to be encouraged to learn and want help.

If you actively look for ways to help your child, you will see
improvements in their learning, but you got to work with
them first. Learning new learning strategies will in itself
help your child.

# Chapter 4

## Attention Deficit Hyperactivity Disorder (ADHD) And Associated Learning Disabilities

When a child's or a person's mind is complex in a web of chaos, it is almost impossible for that person to concentrate. This focus is an essential element required for learning. Many argue that this condition is one of the most common learning disabilities in the world. There are a variety of symptoms, including:

· Difficulty concentrating on tasks or even playing time

· Hearing impairment

· Organizational difficulties

· Short attention span

· Forgetfulness

· Negligence

· Lost property

· Hard to make ends meet

· Explains problems by focusing on the task

· May include hyperactivity

· Difficulty staying in one place for more than an hour

· Excessive motion.

· Fidgety

· Excessive interrupting of others.

· Relentless energy

· Interruptive

To understand how a learning disability is related to this condition, you can break down the symptoms. ADHD, for instance, causes issues with hearing, hand-eye coordination, and other learning-related difficulties like focus and concentration. Since they struggle to learn, we must employ unique strategies to help them.

People with ADHD are frequently prescribed drugs like Ritalin and Adderall by their doctors. These drugs have side effects, but they do work to some extent.

Canada enacted legislation that forbids doctors from prescribing Adderall XR. It was a result of the drug being responsible for several fatalities.

Many of these drugs are more problematic than beneficial. It is of utmost importance and advisable to educate yourself on how to treat this condition with natural herbs and remedies. There are vitamins E, C, and zinc in a common herbal substance called Flavay.

Vitamin C increases the body's need for selenium, while Vitamin E aids the body's promotion of healthy fat cell membranes. It has zinc that helps to support mental health. Concentrated Omega-3 and Spectrient are two additional advantageous herbs. Children can benefit from fish oils as well.

According to many studies, ADHD can start in adolescence and affect people throughout their lives. It is also considered a genetic disease. However, this is not always the case, as many children do not develop symptoms until they are teenagers or adults.

# Dyslexia And Learning Disabilities

Dyslexia is a learning disability that many people suffer from daily. In the past, people diagnosed with disabilities were discharged as stupid, but new research shows that these people have a lot to teach us.

Dyslexia is a brain disorder that impairs a person's ability to interpret language correctly. Some people may perceive words as backward, while others will start writing differently. It makes it difficult for these people to function because it means nothing to them. However, these individuals tend to be good observers.

This condition is another form which gradually misunderstood as a learning disability. The point here is that these people are great learners that need to approach their learning curve differently.

# Schizophrenia

A schizophrenic's mind is in a psychotic state. People with schizophrenia have their own beliefs, and when that line gets crossed, they will make their own rules. If you deviate from their ways, you can put yourself in danger.

Many people with schizophrenia hear voices outside their heads saying, "You're coming for me." These sounds put a person in such a position that they are sure their life is in danger.

A paranoid schizophrenic has a magnificent personality that makes a person want to fight instead of getting angry. In some cases, schizophrenia can cause other people to die because they are scared someone will hurt them.

Now you may be wondering how to teach someone with this disability. These people also have learning disabilities. They are not dumb and don't hallucinate, are attentive to the world around them, and are capable of learning.

But when schizophrenia flares up, it's in their eyes. Their expression seemed lifeless, even a little evil. This situation can make learning become obstructed in their mind through hallucinations and sounds. Disorders are one of the most complex psychological disorders that take a toll on many experts.

There are new drugs that claim to help these psychotic episodes. The problem with some of these teachings today is that people think they are right and you are wrong.

Certain schizophrenics may even believe that you have a master plan to destroy them and that you are their enemy. As a result of the outbreak, many people with the disease are institutionalized, and learning opportunities are often severely limited.

Another problem with teaching such people is that they are very persuasive when not in a psychotic state. They even fooled lie detectors into thinking they were ok and nothing was wrong with them. It is a threat to researchers trying to learn more about the condition.

When a person is in symptom mode, you have better luck getting a wall to talk to you than trying to teach the person anything. It is the only mental illness with a learning disability that prevents learning without medication.

The problem is that many of these people will resist treatment. If you prescribe the wrong medicine, you can put yourself and them in a dangerous situation.

Whether these people can learn does depend on what type of schizophrenia they have. Paranoid schizophrenics are very complex individuals and are difficult to teach. Some researchers believe people can develop schizophrenia without a learning disability, but this is doubtful.

# Dysgraphia, Dyscalculia And Dyspraxia.

There are three primary types of learning disabilities: dysgraphia, dyscalculia, and dyspraxia. Each type affects a different area of learning.

Dysgraphia is a learning disability that affects written expression. People with dysgraphia may have difficulties with spelling, writing, and grammar.

Dyscalculia is a learning disability that affects math skills. People with dyscalculia have difficulty with numbers, calculations, and mathematical concepts.

Dyspraxia is a learning disability that affects the body's immune and nervous systems. People with dyspraxia may have difficulty using scissors, how to plan, and coordinating movement.

# Understanding Auditory Processing Hyperactivity Disorder

Attention Deficit disorder can also be called Auditory Processing Hyperactivity Disorder. It is a difficult situation in which individuals have difficulty understanding and comprehending auditory stimuli.

Therefore, they are hard to learn. Auditory Processing Hyperactivity Disorder is an epidemic that many people suffer from daily.

Auditory processing hyperactivity disorder affects thousands of adults and children. Symptoms usually include:

· Inability to use common sense

· Usually leans forward and talks without worrying about hurting other people's feelings

· Sense of intense boredom

· Impulsive outbursts

· Act before thinking about consequences

· Ignore the consequences of their actions by making excuses for their behaviors

The condition is often active because the cranial nerves that connect the inner ear, which links to the brain and transmit impulses, also control auditory balance and cause learning difficulties.

As APHD progresses, symptoms can expand to include uncontrolled behavior. The problem is that the person's hearing is unbalanced, the central nervous system is overactive, and they lose the ability to think positively or clearly.

It is also important that treatment is consistent to avoid complications. Unfortunately, many people with this disorder turn to alcohol or drugs for relief. Drugs and alcohol can increase suicidal tendencies in these individuals.

In addition, these people do avoid drugs to avoid further problems themselves. Alcohol and drugs can also affect the brain later on and reduces the ability to learn later on.

# Chapter 5

## Health And Wellness Help For Learning Disabilities

People with learning disabilities need to look after themselves physically and mentally. Research shows that regular exercise is a good diet and is critical to maintaining well-balanced learning to improve your skills.

As you work to improve yourself, you realize how much control you have over your mind and body. You can control what you eat, think, feel, and do. You are in control.

If you do not use a list of requirements, there is a high probability that you will struggle to study. Exercise and diet can also reduce our risk of disease and aging.

In addition to maintaining your metabolism and consciousness, a healthy lifestyle can increase your energy levels and help you live longer. Everyone wants to avoid diseases, both mental and physical. Diabetes, high blood pressure, and similar conditions can also cause mental problems that prevent you from studying effectively.

Your body needs healthy levels of carbohydrates, proteins, fats, and other nutrients to produce insulin and maintain normal blood flow. Metabolism plays a role in development because it increases our energy. It is where you want to think about ADHD because the energy produced in these minds can be related to an excessive metabolic rate.

To maintain a healthy metabolism, you must eat healthy foods and get the right amount of energy regularly. The right type of exercise will also help burn off negative energy. Aerobic exercise is good for burning fat and boosting your metabolism. ADHD patients would benefit more from stretching and doing exercises.

Exercise and healthy food can also help rid the body of oxygen. If your oxygen levels are low, this is usually due to impurities in your system. To learn, you need cellular oxygen to cleanse your body and mind.

ADHD is the most common learning disability in the world. The diagnosis of this condition has been around for centuries and is also popular. In the early 1900s, attention deficit disorder was called a "moral deficit." These are considered impulsive behaviors that affect children's ability to learn.

However, these diagnosed people are not stupid, they have a very high level of learning, and they can learn faster and much better in their way than someone else really can.

In other words, a person with ADHD does not need to repeat frequently or focus on one subject for hours. Since people with ADHD have a shorter tonic duration, it makes sense that they require less study time than the average person.

Minimizing tasks for children with ADHD is also very important.

Society tries to demand normality from these children, but pushing them can push them over the edge when not careful. On the other side of this barrier, children below learning levels seem unable to use common sense.

It is where simple things like exercise and diet can help children. Healthy patterns help develop a healthy mind. If children cannot use common sense, they will need structured activities to help them focus on taking control of their lives.

Learning disabilities can be a challenging experience for those living with them. But it doesn't have to be. With the right help, learning disabilities don't have to get in the way of a fulfilling life.

Health and wellness activities are beneficial for people with learning disabilities because they not only help manage the symptoms of the disorder but also increase self-confidence and self-esteem in themselves.

Teachers can help students with learning disabilities in the classroom in several ways. One way is to adjust or change the student's Individualized Education Program (IEP). It may include changing the material presented, allowing extra time for assignments, or using aid.

Another way to help is differentiated instruction, which means tailoring instruction to the needs of each student. It may involve using a different teaching method or delivering the material in another format.

What needs doing here is creating a positive and supportive classroom environment where all students feel safe and respected. Finally, it helps to develop a positive relationship with the family to constant communication about the student's progress.

# Proper Nutrition And Exercise Tips For Those With Learning Disabilities And How To Stay Active

One way to help people with learning disabilities is through proper nutrition. A healthy diet helps improve focus and concentration and provides the nutrients a strong and healthy body needs. Here are a few tips to ensure correct nutrition for people with learning disabilities:

1. Make proper use of a variety of nutrient-dense foods: Eating a variety of nutrient-dense foods helps your body get all the nutrients it needs. Include plenty of fruits, vegetables, whole grains, lean proteins, and low-fat dairy products.

2. You need to limit processed foods and sugary drinks: Too much sugar can lead to hyperactivity and mood swings, and processed foods often lack vital nutrients. Instead, focus on whole, unprocessed foods most of the time.

3. Always get enough protein: Protein is essential for building and repairing tissue and providing energy. Be sure to include lean protein sources such as chicken, fish, beans, lentils, tofu, eggs, and nuts.

If you have a learning disability, it can be difficult for you to exercise and stay active. However, physical activity has many benefits, including improved mental health and increased energy levels. Here are some tips to get you started.

1. Talk to your doctor before you start doing a new exercise routine. It is of utmost importance if you have a medical condition that can be affected by physical activity.

2. Set realistic goals for yourself. Start small and gradually increase the amount of time or intensity level as you feel comfortable.

3. Choose an activity that you enjoy a lot and then fits your lifestyle. Walking, swimming, and cycling are good rewarding options that you can easily do at your own pace.

4. Find a workout partner or join a group class to stay motivated. It helps to work out with someone who can make exercising more fun and help you stick with it in the long run.

5. Always warm up before the exercise and cool down afterwards to avoid injury. Prepare your body for action by stretching or doing light aerobic exercising like walking on the spot.

6. Listen to your body and take breaks when necessary. If you feel sore or overtired, stop and rest until you feel better before continuing with the exercise you were doing.

7. Drink plenty of water: Staying hydrated is essential for everyone's health, but the amount of water a person needs depends on climate, clothing, and the intensity and duration of exercise.

# Disabilities That Hinder Learning And Working Through Them

Learning is a slow process that we tried to understand over the years. Many people have gifted minds and can understand many areas of study, while others can specialize in certain subjects and struggle. Some people may be good at English but bad at math, while others are the opposite.

For example, a woman who left school earlier than most and had children earlier may not have had the best formal education, but she has seen life and learned to live up to her level of education. In other words, she does learn from observation and experience. This woman can be clever as a whip and manage her money well.

As you can see, everyone learns differently. Education is good, but sometimes education lacks reality. Most teachers are good, but many can't do more and won't be able to help you.

Teachers often struggle to help people reach their level of understanding, and sometimes teachers find it hard to get a child's level of thinking. Some teachers are also often difficult to understand. Several instructors don't care at all.

It should encourage other people with learning disabilities not to give up. They should consider all options given to them. It is of utmost importance not to let yourself down.

If you or your child is struggling, it is wise to have a mind-body assessment. Once you come to understand the problem, you will be better and will be able to move forward.


When you have a disorder like ADHD, make sure you understand the deeper meaning of the condition. You must understand what is happening in your body and how you react. Once you've tested with medication, be prepared to argue if you don't feel you need it. Tell them you want to explore other options.

# Overcoming Mental Health Issues By Finding The Right Resources And Support

Mental health problems are widespread and affect millions of people worldwide. According to the World Health Organization, one in four people will experience mental health problems at some point in their entire life. But despite their prevalence, mental illnesses are often under diagnosed and under treated.

There are many reasons why mental health problems go undiagnosed. Sometimes people hesitate to seek help because of the stigma associated with mental illness. Others may not realize they have a problem or may not believe therapy will help.

Mental health issues can be hard to overcome, but they are possible with the right help. Learning disabilities can make it very difficult to deal with mental health problems because they can make it difficult to understand and process information. However, there are ways to overcome these difficulties.

With reliable support, people with learning disabilities can cope with their mental health problems like anyone else. There are many different types of support everyone needs depending on their circumstances.

Some people may need medication to help them manage their symptoms, while others may benefit from therapy or counseling. If you are struggling with mental health issues, it is vital to seek professional help.

There is no one-size-fits-all solution to coping with mental health problems. However, some resources and types of support can be helpful for many people. The most important thing is to find what works best for you and stick to it.

It is especially true if your symptoms interfere with your ability to perform daily activities. A mental health professional can assess your situation and recommend a detailed plan tailored to you. They can also provide the resources and support you need to overcome your challenges.

It can be overwhelming if you or your child is diagnosed with a learning disability. There are so many unknowns that it can feel like you don't know where to turn.

No matter what resources and support you find, it's important to remember that progress takes time. Be patient, and don't give up when things get tough. With perseverance, you can overcome mental problems and live a fulfilling life.

The good news is that there are plenty of resources and support to help you navigate this new journey. Here are some tips for finding the right help for you or your child:
1. Talk to your doctor or nurse. They should be able to provide you with some resources and information about learning disabilities.

2. Contact a local support group. They can be a great way to connect with other families with learning disabilities for people going through similar experiences. It can provide a sense of community and allow you to share your struggles and triumphs with others who understand what you are

going through.

3. Check out specialized schools or programs. Some schools offer programs specifically for students with learning disabilities. If your child is struggling in a traditional school setting, this may be the solution for your child.

4. Talk to a mental health professional. They can provide guidance and support if you or your child is struggling with a learning disability diagnosis.

5. Finding the right therapist or counselor is an important step. You will feel comfortable talking about your deepest thoughts and feelings. They can help you understand your thoughts and feelings and help you healthily deal with them.

6. Take advantage of online resources and social media groups. There are a lot of reliable websites and online forums that provide the necessary support and required information about learning disabilities.

7. It is important to note that the resources and support most helpful for mental health differ from person to person. What works for one may not work for another. The important thing is to find what works best for you and be open to trying new things.

# Conclusion

From the day you are born, you can see, hear, smell, touch even empathize with those around you. A newborn baby can even sense when his mother is near him. The child also can detect his mother's emotions. Therefore, the child's learning process begins in the mother's womb.

When a child is taken care of by their mother with bipolar depression, the child will follow the mother's example and behave irrationally. If the father is an alcoholic, the child may learn to drink to calm down when threatened.

If the child is depressed, he may even turn to alcohol. A child may even believe that happiness should be punishable. All these behaviors are how children view their parents as role models.

What a child hears and sees is an example of how a child grows. A child adapts to their environment and their behavior to survive. It does not necessarily mean that children raised in dysfunctional homes will be able to learn, but it does put them at risk of disabilities later in life.

In reality, people who are isolated suffer tremendously more than others. When children reach preschool or elementary age, they meet new people who set new rules for them in life.

Rules can influence a child's life and teach them that it is good to be happy and bad to act irrationally. Every adult's influence on a child's life touches them positively and negatively. We hope it is positive.

But when the rules children learn at school conflict with what they get at home, confusion can arise. If mom behaves irrationally and suffers from manic-depressive disorders, but dad drinks a lot in times of stress, then children see conflicts in their lives and don't know who to believe.

They don't know if it's good or not to be ecstatic and what's going on in life. A child may see their dad go to the bottle temporarily to relieve stress, and the child may believe that happiness is an illusion.

So what happens when the kids go back to school? The child sees the rules learned at school and compares these rules with what the parents show the child at home.

A child can see school as a "fictional land" and home as a harsh reality. But the child is then forced to compare two conflicting rules in their life. They see happy schools and not-so-happy homes. Where is the child's faith?

Children's opinions are rare because everyone teaches children different things. They learn to believe by agreeing with other people. A perfect example of a child who is confused is a child who grew up in a poor home, as shown below.

The child grows up in a family whose mother is a paranoid schizophrenic and is "beaten" by a man she calls her husband. A mother teaches her child that boys are better than girls, and the child believes it. The mother also told the child that she only be seen and not heard. Parents sometimes even see children as a waste of time.

The father taught the child that talking, crying, and even feeling overly happy are not good, and she would get in trouble for any of them. The child is afraid of the father and is afraid to express her feelings. If she frustrates him, logically or illogically, she gets punished.

They teach young children that education is worthless and the only value of education is that a method used to control other people's lives. In that sense, the man is spot on that the National Education Association is to govern rather than focus on helping children learn.

Later, as the child grows up, the child sees other children harming, imitating, criticizing, and hurting others. The child watched while the teacher stood by and punished the children who had acted against the bullying. Children observe leaders and their behavior when they ask difficult questions.

Now this woman can learn to behave like those around her. However, she had her views and decided to stick to them. As you can see, a child who is now an adult is struggling with life and complications that hinder her ability to learn.

However, the woman learned that by observing, comparing, contrasting, analyzing, and investigating, she learned to look for facts that would justify her views on life. It is the life of many children with learning disabilities.

Of course, not all children will live in poverty, but they will see a conflict between family morals and school values. They are either defeated by confusion or pushed on.

Children with the disorder were more likely to develop other forms of mental illness or deficit. As a result, they may develop learning disabilities. Other children may also have only one or more learning difficulties. Some children will be determined to fight the disorder, while others will give up.

Learning disabilities are sometimes frustrating but also a demanding problem to manage when you don't know how, but with the right strategies and support, students can succeed in the classroom.

Teachers have tremendous potential to help students with learning disabilities reach their full potential through a blend of accommodations, research-backed interventions, and individualized lesson plans tailored to each student's strengths and needs.

As you can see, by using these strategies, educators can create an environment where all students feel empowered and supported to succeed when they receive the correct instruction they need.

Learning disabilities can significantly affect a person's ability to learn and grow. Parents, educators, and health professionals must understand the symptoms of learning disabilities to provide appropriate support and resources.

By understanding the signs of learning disabilities, we can help make matters much easier for people with learning disabilities to get the help they need to reach their full potential.

Learning disabilities are a complex and widespread problem that can significantly affect academic performance. A diagnosis of a learning disability is made by assessing a person's academic performance regarding cognitive ability and can be adjusted for age and level of education.

Several strategies and approaches can help understand and manage learning disabilities. By understanding the signs of learning disabilities, educators can take steps to create an inclusive classroom environment that meets the needs of all students.

In addition, parents should also be aware of the difficulties their children may face so that they can seek appropriate strategies to provide educational support. With early intervention and diagnosis, children with learning disabilities can succeed in school and life.

What happens to you or your child is entirely up to you. You can learn more, do the research you need, and fight the disability. Or you can submit to the disability and do nothing. However, you must understand that it is possible to overcome these obstacles and learn as much as you want.

**PS:** I hope this book did more than inspire you but also broadened your perspective on learning disabilities. All children are a true blessing and an extraordinary gift from our Heavenly Father. Let us cherish them forever.

**Kind regards and blessings.**

**Glenn Smit**

9 798223 024385